BRIGHT IDEA BOOKS

PARK
Naturalist

by Lisa Harkrader

CAPSTONE PRESS
a capstone imprint

Bright Idea Books are published by Capstone Press
1710 Roe Crest Drive, North Mankato, Minnesota 56003
www.mycapstone.com

Copyright © 2019 by Capstone Press, a Capstone imprint. All rights reserved. No part of this publication may be reproduced in whole or in part, or stored in a retrieval system, or transmitted in any form or by any means, electronic, mechanical, photocopying, recording, or otherwise, without written permission of the publisher.

Library of Congress Cataloging-in-Publication Data
Names: Harkrader, Lisa, author.
Title: Park naturalist / by Lisa Harkrader.
Description: North Mankato, Minnesota : Bright Idea Books, an imprint of
    Capstone Press, [2019] | Series: Jobs with animals | Audience: Age 9-12. |
    Audience: Grade 4 to 6. | Includes bibliographical references and index.
Identifiers: LCCN 2018035988 | ISBN 9781543557855 (hardcover : alk. paper) |
    ISBN 9781543558173 (ebook) | ISBN 9781543560473 (paperback)
Subjects: LCSH: Natural history--Vocational guidance--Juvenile literature. |
    Park naturalists--Vocational guidance--Juvenile literature.
Classification: LCC QH49 .H37 2019 | DDC 508.023--dc23
LC record available at https://lccn.loc.gov/2018035988

Editorial Credits
Editor: Meg Gaertner
Designer: Becky Daum
Production Specialist: Dan Peluso

Photo Credits
iStockphoto: AriciaMartinez, 22–23, FatCamera, 30–31, guenterguni, 27, KeithBinns, 28,
PamelaJoeMcFarlane, 21, Peopleimages, cover, Silvrshootr, 9, sshepard, 12–13, wanderluster,
24–25; Shutterstock Images: danm12, 6, Don Mammoser, 10–11, 26, Gudkov Andrey, 11, Jim
Feliciano, 5, Rob Crandall, 15, Tupungato, 16–17, Wandel Guides, 6–7, 18–19

TABLE OF CONTENTS

CHAPTER 1

PARK
Naturalist

The school bus pulls up at the park. Students get off the bus. A woman in a park uniform greets them. She leads the students through the park. The woman tells the students about park **wildlife**. She talks about the plants. The woman is a park naturalist.

Parks can include the ruins of homes and cities where people lived long ago.

A WILDLIFE EXPERT

A park naturalist is a kind of **park ranger**. Park naturalists know about the wildlife in the park. They teach people about the wildlife. They also teach people about the park.

Naturalists might teach visitors about the park's snakes.

Some parks have "ambassador" animals. These animals can interact with visitors.

Do you like animals and nature? Maybe a job as a park naturalist is for you.

CHAPTER 2

THE Work

Park naturalists love the outdoors. That is a good thing. They spend a lot of time there! They work in **national parks**. They learn all about their parks. They learn plant and animal names. They learn where the plants and animals live.

Park naturalists care about nature. They protect the land. They protect the plants and animals. They teach park visitors how to protect nature.

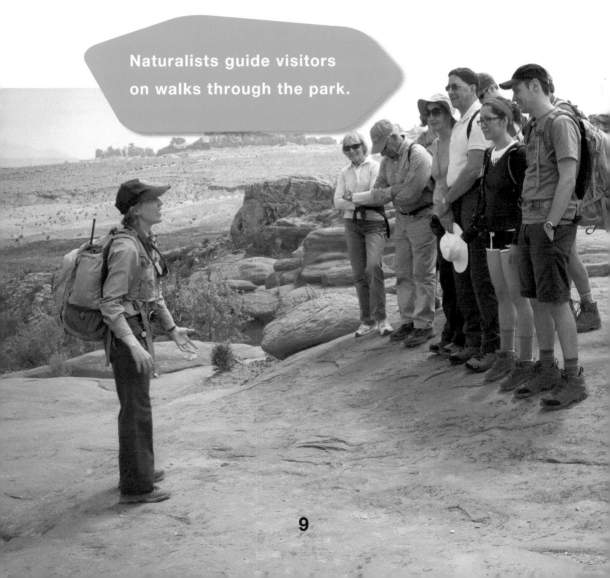

Naturalists guide visitors on walks through the park.

A naturalist at Komodo National Park in Indonesia leads visitors to the burrow of a komodo dragon.

YEAR-ROUND JOB

Park naturalists work in all kinds of weather. It can rain or snow. They still may have outside work to do.

Many people come to parks. Families and clubs visit. Students come on field trips. Park naturalists tell visitors about the park. They teach in many ways. They give talks. They lead hikes. They tell visitors about the wildlife they see. They point out interesting things in the park.

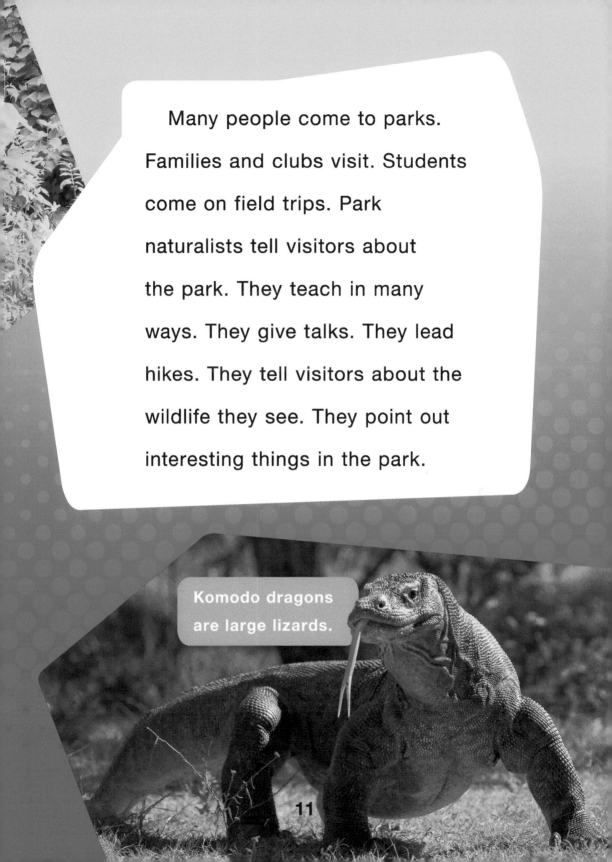

Komodo dragons are large lizards.

THE GREAT INDOORS

Park naturalists have indoor jobs too. Sometimes they work in a park's visitor center. They plan activities for park visitors. They answer questions for visitors. They give out maps of the park.

Park naturalists also make displays. They make handouts and videos. These resources tell about the local wildlife. They tell about the park's history.

People can get information about the park from the park's visitor center.

CHAPTER 3

THE
Workplace

Park naturalists work in many kinds of parks. Many of them work in national parks. A national park is run by a nation's government. These parks keep the land safe. They keep the wildlife safe. They give people a place to enjoy nature.

A naturalist gives a tour at Mesa Verde National Park in Colorado.

The United States has 417 national park sites. All of the parks are different. Some parks are **marshlands**. Some are seashores. Some are forests. The different parks have different kinds of wildlife.

YELLOWSTONE

Yellowstone was the first national park in the United States. It covers parts of Montana, Wyoming, and Idaho.

Utah's Arches National Park is a rocky desert.

17

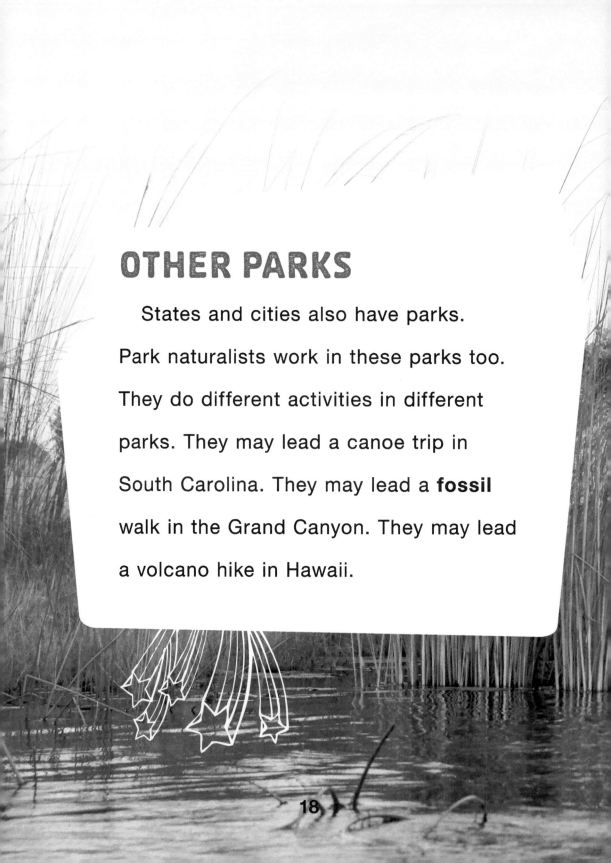

OTHER PARKS

States and cities also have parks. Park naturalists work in these parks too. They do different activities in different parks. They may lead a canoe trip in South Carolina. They may lead a **fossil** walk in the Grand Canyon. They may lead a volcano hike in Hawaii.

Some park areas are best reached by boat.

CHAPTER 4

GETTING the Job

Do you want to be a park naturalist? The first step is to go to school. Park naturalist jobs require a college degree. Some positions call for more education. People study subjects that help them work in parks. They study science. They study wildlife. They study how to run a park.

A class visits the local park to learn about mushrooms.

GETTING EXPERIENCE

You can learn a lot outside of school too. People can become **interns**. Interns work at a park for a short time. They gain work skills.

VOLUNTEERING

Many people **volunteer** at parks. Volunteering is a good way to learn about parks.

Interns can learn from park naturalists.

People who visit Yellowstone in the less popular winter months can see steaming **geysers** on their trip.

ON THE JOB

Most parks are not busy all year. They are busy only in some seasons. Some park naturalists work only during busy seasons. They are called **seasonal** workers.

Most park naturalists make $30,000 to $60,000 per year. Managers can make $80,000 per year. Part-time and seasonal workers make about $15 per hour.

Naturalists get to teach others about wildlife.

Most park naturalists like their jobs. They get to spend a lot of time in nature. They get to work with wildlife. They get to meet new people. They do new things every day.

Naturalists get to share their love of nature with visitors.

GLOSSARY

fossil
the remains of an animal or plant that lived a long time ago

geyser
a hot spring of water that sometimes boils, sending a tall column of water into the air

intern
a student or trainee who works for a short time to gain new skills

marshland
wet, low-lying land

national park
an area of the countryside protected by the federal government

park ranger
a person who protects national, state, and local parks

seasonal
limited to a season of the year

volunteer
to work or help out without being paid

wildlife
the animals that live in a region

OTHER JOBS TO CONSIDER

GAME WARDEN

Game wardens enforce hunting, fishing, and boating laws. They usually work in parks, forests, and recreation areas.

WILDLIFE BIOLOGIST

Wildlife biologists are scientists. They watch animals in the wild. They study animals' behavior. They see how animals live in the wild.

WILDLIFE MANAGER

Wildlife managers solve problems related to wildlife. They protect animals from human activity. They also make sure people can enjoy wildlife safely.

ACTIVITY

LEARN AND TEACH

Choose an outdoor place near your home or school. Choose a park. Choose a playground. You can even choose your own backyard.

Watch the wildlife and look at the plants in the outdoor place. What kinds of plants live there? What kinds of animals live there? How do they behave? Make notes or sketches. You can even take pictures.

Now use your notes, sketches, and pictures to make a poster or handout. Show your poster or handout to your friends and family. Your poster or handout will teach other people about the wildlife you saw.

FURTHER RESOURCES

Interested in becoming a park naturalist? Learn more here:

Carson, Mary Kay. *Park Scientists: Gila Monsters, Geysers, and Grizzly Bears in America's Own Backyard*. Boston, Mass.: Houghton Mifflin Harcourt, 2014.

National Park Service: Junior Rangers Program
www.nps.gov/kids/jrRangers.cfm

Want to know more about national parks? Check out these resources:

National Geographic Kids: National Parks
https://kids.nationalgeographic.com/explore/nature/national-parks/

Wallace, Audra. *Yellowstone*. New York: Scholastic Inc, 2018.

Winterberg, Jenna. *Parks for All: U.S. National Parks*. Huntington Beach, Calif.: Teacher Created Materials, 2017.

INDEX